FISHING

fishing

AN ANGLER'S DICTIONARY

BY HENRY BEARD
& ROY McKIE

METHUEN

Original edition first published in the United States of America

This revised edition first published in Great Britain in 1985 by Methuen London, Michelin House, 81 Fulham Road, London SW3 6RB

Text and illustrations
Copyright © 1983, 1985 by Henry Beard and Roy McKie

A CIP catalogue record of this book is available from the British Library

ISBN 0–413–68260–9

AUTHORS' NOTE

The authors are grateful for the advice given to them by David Burnett during the preparation of the Methuen edition of this book

Made and printed in Great Britain
by Redwood Books, Trowbridge, Wilts

To all those who have heard the call of the fish.

Aquarium

A

Advice	Two or more pieces of contradictory angling information contained in a single phrase or sentence.
Angling	The art of fishing, as practised by those who seek to catch fish not for profit or for food, but rather for the sport involved. The commonly accepted source of the term "angling" is an ancient Indo-European word, *anka*, meaning "hook" or "to fish with a hook," but several other words are also likely candidates, including *enka* ("unwise expenditure" or "useless task"); *unglo* ("one who is tormented by insects"); *onku* ("loud or frequent lamentation"); *angi* ("to deceive"); *onklo* ("possession by demons"); and *angla* ("love of pointless suffering").
Aquarium	Glass-walled enclosure for the display of fish. Although some fishermen do keep fish as pets, this hobby is not recommended for anyone even faintly interested in angling, as the urge to match wits with a finny quarry, however tame, is eventually bound to overcome other considerations. Aquariums with bulletproof glass and locked lids, such as the bulky but impenetrable "Fish Fort" or the armoured "Centurion Fish Tank" are available, but, frankly, fishermen will spare themselves much trouble if they simply select some other avocation equally well suited to their temperaments but less fraught with disturbing temptation, such as roller-skating, collecting string, or raising bees.
Artificial	Type of synthetic bait rejected by a finicky fish because it is too large or too small, or because it has the wrong shape, bears the wrong colouration, or makes the wrong motions in the water. *See* NATURAL.

Bait Casting

Atlantic	Ocean that separates a large segment of the English-speaking fishing population into two distinct subgroups: the gregarious, flashy American fisherman and the drab, solitary British angler. Both are characterised by elaborate tales, shifty eyes, and generally unreliable scales.

B

Bailiff	Official who enforces local fish and game laws. These vary from place to place: in Wales, for example, a hook may not be baited with anything whose name in Welsh rhymes with "ddmllwr"; in Scotland, it is against the law to make change or quote scripture within 1,000 yards of a stream; and in Ireland it is a crime to talk politics in a skiff.
Baffling	*1. n.* Compartmentalised interior construction of a down-filled sleeping bag. *2. adj.* Perplexing or puzzling, as in a baffling problem involving a sleeping bag, such as how to put a mass of bedding the size of a small pony into a receptacle designed to hold shaving articles.
Bait Casting	Angling method developed in the nineteenth century whose basic component is a revolving reel that must be carefully controlled by hand. Because of the danger of the line outrunning the reel and becoming tangled, bait-casting outfits are tricky to use. Nevertheless, many anglers find in that deficiency a desirable feature, since the sight of a reel festooned with loops of knotted fishing line renders their gear virtually theftproof, eliminates any interest fellow anglers might have had in borrowing it, and magically discourages requests for fishing information or assistance.

Bamboo Eye-pleasing, but expensive type of rod, used primarily by anglers who fish for compliments.

Bamboozle To persuade an angler to purchase a bamboo fishing rod.

Barnacle The only marine species whose successful accumulation in large numbers on a deep-sea fishing boat can be accepted on the basis of an unverified oral report.

Barracuda Jocular term for operator of a boat-charter company.

Basking Shark *1.* A large, plankton-eating fish of the species Ceterhinus. *2.* A bookmaker on a seaside holiday in Spain.

Bass Sporting sea fish eagerly sought by salt-water anglers. It is also favoured by Chinese chefs, and non-fishermen interested in getting a taste both of the fish and of the pointless, mind-numbing toil involved in catching it can easily do so in the nearest Chinese restaurant by attempting to eat a whole unboned sea bass with chopsticks.

Beach A narrow strip of sand, gravel, or stone that is located between a large body of water in which there are no fish and a large stretch of land in which there are no pubs.

Bedrock *1.* Type of stream bottom consisting of bare rock. *2.* Bothersome stony object found under sleeping bags.

Billfish An informal term for any of the large salt-water game fishes, such as the sailfish and swordfish, whose upper jaws extend into sharp spears. They are called billfish because, following a day's outing in search of one of these magnificent creatures, the captain of a boat traditionally presents the angler who chartered her with an enormous bill in a short, but emotional dockside ceremony.

Barracuda

Bite

Bite	The act of a fish taking something into its mouth. As a rule, the eagerness of an angler for a fish to bite is in inverse proportion to his distance from its jaws.
Blue Marlin	Highly prized and difficult-to-catch salt-water game fish.
Blue Moon	Period during which blue marlin may be caught.
Bonefish	Skittish, much-sought-after game fish found in shallow-water "flats" in Florida, the Bahamas, and the Caribbean. Bonefishing can be a gruelling and nerve-wracking sport for the fisherman, but it is exciting and enjoyable to watch, and spectators often pause to take in the action as the angler goes through an amazing series of unpredictable movements, ranging from tooth-jarring slaps as a sandfly finds its target on a sunburned neck to breathtaking leaps as a piece of sharp coral pierces a shoe. And once in a while, onlookers may be lucky enough to witness a sensational run when a small ground shark or poisonous ray sends the startled bonefisherman into a flurry of rapid strides and jerky hops, and he churns the water white in a mad dash for dry land, filling the tropical air with a burst of language of unforgettable richness and colour.
Bream	Large, abundant fish that is often the quarry in match-fishing, a vile perversion of the purity of angling in which fishermen compete for sums of money awarded for the biggest catch or make wagers on the day's outcome. The crude thrill of so mercenary a pursuit simply does not compare to the subtle pleasure enjoyed by the true sportsman who, unaffected by crass monetary considerations, stands in a tranquil trout stream, lost in peaceful reverie, idly planning new methods of fiddling his expense account or cheating the Inland Revenue.

Brook Trout	Breed of native trout that was common in American rivers before the hordes of European brown trout were introduced in the 1880s, but which are now usually only found in the headwaters of the better private streams. They are aggravatingly choosy fish, and are easily put off by loud, flashy lures tied with synthetic substances such as polyester or tinsel, and about the only chance of taking one is with a lightly gin-soaked "very dry fly" tied in a conservative plaid or tattersall pattern.
Bucket	Clumsy form of metallic footgear found on fishing boats.
Bug	*1.* Large surface lure. *2.* Individual who is crazy about fishing. *3.* Insect that is crazy about *2.*

C

Camera	Small, but quite heavy object used by anglers to store small amounts of water and a canister of spoiled film.
Camp	As used by fishermen, a term denoting the place where the outboard motor broke.
Can	The only place where salmon are sure to be found with any degree of certainty.
Cane Pole	The simplest fishing rig, consisting of a long stick with a length of line permanently attached to its tip. It is a common bit of fishing lore among the uninitiated that a barefoot boy equipped with such a pole and using a bent pin for a hook and worms for bait will invariably go home with more fish than an expensively outfitted angler. This is arrant nonsense. There is simply no substitute for the

Bugs

Carp

subtlety of mind and singleness of purpose of the dedicated bait caster or fly fisherman. Perhaps he flashes a bogus, but convincing, game warden badge and confiscates the little rascal's lucky catch; maybe he places a fatherly hand lightly on the lad's shoulder and speaks firmly, yet kindly, of the horrors of the reform school that await truants apprehended by a concerned citizen and delivered to the proper authorities; or it could be that he simply offers a tantalising "dough ball" of wadded bank notes to the dimwitted adolescent, suggesting in an offhand manner some of the cavity-producing delicacies that might take the place of a tiresome meal of salmon or trout. But whatever his methods, the experienced angler will always get the fish, for a youth's crude skill is no match for his cunning.

Canoe	Long, narrow, sharp-ended boat in which the typical lake fisherman passes through the most dramatic portion of the metamorphosis that began with his emergence from his cocoonlike sleeping bag at dawn. At first huddling in the unfamiliar craft as he adjusts to his new environment, he rises unsteadily to his feet, extends his fishing rod, and then goes into a brief flying phase, followed by a long aquatic or swimming stage.
Carp	Plentiful, tasty, and very game fish that is a favourite of anglers who lack access to trout streams like the Test, the Wye, the Wharfe, the Avon, the Exe, the Eden, and the Ribble. Because carp have a high tolerance for polluted waters, they provide fine, if messy, sport in lesser rivers such as the Stye, the Wen, the Sloven, the Pest, the Frowst, the Draff, the Ort, the Lees, the Slubber, the Drivel, the Dross, the Midden, and the Mixen.

Char

Catch-and-release	*1.* Term for stretch of public stream where fish caught must be released alive. *2.* Term for stretch of private stream where trespassers caught are released after a lecture, a series of threats, and a brief introduction to a large dog.
Catfish	Peculiar-looking fresh and salt-water fish species that can grow to an absolutely enormous size. Anglers often boast of the giants they have caught in moats, canals, or inshore shallows, but the Soviet Ministry of Fishing claims the record for the largest one ever captured, a several-thousand-ton, 350-foot monster taken in tow by a Russian trawler off the Karlskrona naval base in Sweden.
Char	*1.* Group of fishes, including the lake and brook trout, which are related both to salmon and to other trout. *2.* Common method of cooking *1* over a campfire.
Cheese	Surprisingly effective bait the use of which is frowned upon by dedicated anglers who find it most unsporting, and who prefer the time-honoured technique of using artificial lures that imitate the natural insect food consumed by fish. Many anglers compromise and combine efficiency with tradition by strictly confining themselves to native cheeses, which they fashion into fanciful shapes that mimic flies and bugs—Blue Vinny, Royal Gloucester, Cheddar Midge, and Edam's Fancy are just a few of the popular patterns. Another much-favoured approach is to employ a hybrid lure consisting of a conventional dry or wet fly and a surreptitiously applied gob of cheese. This method is particularly effective when hypercritical fly fishermen are angling in the immediate vicinity, for it takes a sharp eye to spot the dairy product in a Krafty Devil, Cheshire Googly, or Stilton Bosey.

Club

Chub	Numerous and sizeable river fish. Sadly, it has bland, mushy flesh and seven hundred and ninety million bones.
Chum	*1.* Fish heads or innards, raw clams, smelly garbage, and the like, which are chopped up and thrown over the side of a salt-water fishing vessel to attract game fish. *2.* Friendly fellow angler who will chop up fish heads and innards, raw clams, smelly garbage and the like and throw them over the side for you while you concentrate on keeping a recently eaten meal in its proper location.
Club	*1.* Long bar of wood used to render fish senseless. *2.* Place with a long bar of wood where fishermen go to render themselves senseless.
Cockle	Tasty but not very aggressive marine animal obtained through a rather slow-paced form of fishing that combines the entertainment value of hunting for a lost spectacle case with the sporting qualities of coal-mining.
Cod	Game fish usually taken from party boats in ocean waters during winter months. The most critical part of cod fishing occurs long before the fishing grounds are reached. This is the all-important "rise," which takes place in the dark at about 5 A.M. when the dramatic "strike" of the alarm clock turns the motionless, quiescent angler into a thrashing, seething mass of elbows and bedclothes and sends him into a heart-stopping "leap." If at this point the clock is thrown sharply across the room with an abrupt, powerful arm stroke, then chances are that the angler is about to enter a prolonged dormant phase, and there is little hope that cod will be taken that day.
Conger Eel	Three feet of murderous cat food with a mangle on the end.

Corrosion Resistant	Term found on articles of fishing equipment indicating that they are capable of withstanding the harmful effects of salt-water exposure for 91, 181, or 366 days, depending on the nature of the guarantee.
Creel	Lightweight, easily carried wickerwork basket in which the day's catch is placed.
Creep	Angler who insists on examining the contents of another fisherman's creel.
Custom-made	Bilked to order.

D

Dace	Common minnow with a spindle-shaped body. Along with tench, barbel, rudd, roach, carp, bream, chub, perch, and gudgeon, dace are classified as coarse fish, and while it is true that these species lack the noble qualities of the superior breeds of salmon and trout and that some of them have undesirable habits, like digging up and eating salmon eggs, uprooting aquatic plants, and crowding out more desirable fish, the "citizens" of our English rivers are for the most part well behaved. Alas, this is not true of their American cousins, a few of which have been inadvertently introduced into British streams, and fishermen who hear vulgar spitting noises when they cast, have their lures stolen or snagged, find their lines tied together, or are "teased" unmercifully with false strikes have probably encountered a Texan raunch, a Florida ruck, a New York lout, a Georgia wrawl, a California churl, a Midwestern mucker, or a New England cad.

Dry Flies (Basic Patterns)

CUTHBERTSON

INFALLIBLE

IMPROVED DIRECTOR

WHIRLING DEVIL

CARSON'S FANCY

HACKLE PRINCE

LUCKY LADY

MARCH QUILL

DUSTY DEVIL

QUEEN OF THE MAY

MCGILLICUDDY

PARSON'S OATH

GORDON'S GLORY

FERNANDA

REDUCED DAISY MILLER

ROYAL FOOTMAN

GIBB'S VARIANT

SOUTH FORK SPECIAL

INVINCIBLE

STRAW DOG

GOSSAMER GHOST

Dolphin	Aggressive tropical game fish that is a true fish, and is in no way related to the playful, intelligent, and often helpful aquatic mammal, the porpoise. The confusion between the two names is based on a superficial similarity in the shape of their snouts and not on any shared beneficial behavioural traits, as shipwrecked sailors learn to their dismay when the dull-witted, but malevolent dolphins push them off their rafts, eat their life jackets, and nudge them out to sea.
Dope	*1.* Any fluid applied to a dry fly to make it float. *2.* Any individual who applies this substance to a wet fly.
Dry Flies	Fly-fishing lure designed to float on the surface of the water. There are many different kinds, and they are hard to tell apart, but they all fit into one of six basic categories: Mashed, Bent, Slimy, Hairless, Hookless, and Hopeless.
Dun	*1.* Second stage in development on rivers of the mayfly. *2.* Second stage in purchase on credit of fishing gear.
Dusk	Brief twilight period that separates the time when fish don't bite because they can see the line from the time when fish don't bite because they can't see the lure.

E

Earthworm	There are probably as many different lures as there are fishermen, but none is more universally effective in catching freshwater fish than that old stand-by, the earthworm. Worms can be bought from bait shops in most fishing areas, but many anglers prefer to raise their own to assure themselves of a plentiful and virtually cost-free supply. This is not difficult to do. Worms are easily collected from a garden after heavy rain, and may be stored

for long periods in a cool, dark place in a box filled with damp shredded newspaper, moistened leaves, wet moss, or some similar bedding material, with a little corn meal or powdered milk thrown in for food. But a word of warning: anglers are by nature sweet-tempered and sensitive, and they often go overboard, constructing elaborate houses with individual beds for their night crawlers and naming favourite worms. This is not a good idea, for when the time comes to pop Esmeralda into a bait can or slip a hook through Reginald, the tearful fisherman may find that he lacks the heart to bid farewell to his wriggling friends.

Exaggeration   Formal term for a collection of fishermen, i.e., an *exaggeration* of anglers.

F

False Cast   *1.* Technique used by fly fishermen after an unsatisfactory cast to straighten a kinked line and increase its velocity. *2.* Strap-on plaster device worn to work by sly fishermen after an unexplained absence to strengthen a weak line and improve its credibility.

Fathom   *1. n.* Measurement of ocean depth, often made on fishing boats with an electronic sounding device called a fathometer. *2. v.* To comprehend, as in, "I cannot fathom why I paid £500 for a malfunctioning electronic device that does nothing but smoke and squeak."

Fighting Chair   Elaborate, swivel-mounted seat in the stern of a sea-going charter boat in which a salt-water fisherman struggles with his overpowering urge to order the captain to turn around and return to port.

False Cast

Fish	The only living creature in any given stretch of stream, river, lake, or bay that doesn't have a hook in it and isn't smoking a pipe.
Fish and Chips	A dish consisting of fried potatoes and pieces of fried fish. Normally, the fish used is Iceland haddock or rock salmon, but in unscrupulous shops it is likely to be roof trout (pigeon), spring cod (kangaroo), saddle bass (horse), or lawn flounder (squirrel).

Fish Story

The use of non-standard terms for the estimated size of a fish that eluded capture has tended to unnecessarily undermine the veracity of well-meaning anglers. Adherence to the internationally recognised Rules for Reporting Lost Fish will not only eliminate possible confusion or misinterpretation, but will also go far toward improving the overall credibility of anglers everywhere:

FLASH OF SCALES UNDER WATER: Lunker
SLIGHT RIPPLE: Bruiser
AUDIBLE SPLASH: Whopper
PERCEPTIBLE NIBBLE: Giant
HARD TUG ON LINE: Monster
MISSING LURE OR SNAPPED LEADER: Leviathan
BROKEN LINE: Behemoth
LOST ROD: Fishzilla.

Fishing Trip	Journey undertaken by one or more anglers to a place where no one can remember when it has rained so much.
Fluke	*1.* Summer flounder. *2.* Catching a summer flounder.
Fly Box	*1.* Plastic or metal container for storing flies. *2.* To exchange blows in a sparring contest with any of the two-winged insects of the order Diptera. Fishermen are generally not belligerent individuals, but it's common to

Fish Story (Presentation of the Evidence)

see them engaged in a furious bout with a huge fly, bobbing and weaving and making quick jabs and thrusts at what seems to be thin air. Shrewd onlookers invariably put their money on the insect, favouring its agility, speed, and staying power over the angler's size, weight, and ability to absorb punishment, much of it self-inflicted, and these aerial featherweights seldom disappoint their backers.

Fly Casting

This is the most elegant, but also the most demanding form of freshwater fishing, because unlike other casting methods, in fly fishing it is the line itself rather than the lure at the end of it that is cast toward the target, and 30 or more feet of casting line must be stripped off the reel and set into controlled motion overhead with precise, whiplike movements of the rod. Accurate fly casting is very difficult to master, but it appeals to fishermen who prefer finesse to force and measure their success as much in the quality of the cast as in the quantity of the catch. Such a fisherman, standing in a crystal chalkstream, is the very epitome of the sportsman, as he carefully gauges the wind and water and instinctively makes a hundred minor but crucial calculations. He moves the supple rod back and forth in an easy rhythm, and the faintly whispering line describes subtle parabolas in the air, the infinitesimal fly dancing at its tip, the hook sparkling in the sun. At last, with a final graceful overhead stroke, he shoots the delicate loops through the air. Time stands still. And then a weird, almost animal cry shatters the silence as a well-honed barb bites into the posterior of an angler just downstream. Now comes the elemental test of a fly fisherman's mettle. Without a moment's hesitation, he cuts his line, nimbly makes his way to the stream bank, scoops up his gear, and deposits it in his car with a

Fly Casting (Public Stream)

practised flick of the wrist. Then, with deft hand motions perfected by long practice, he turns on the ignition, spins the wheel, and speeds away. Is he disappointed? No, for he'll soon fish again—in another county—and he has the satisfaction of knowing that, in a fellow angler's fish story, he's the one that got away.

Flying Fish	*1.* Remarkable tropical fish capable of skimming over the waves for 100 feet or more on tiny winglike fins. *2.* Any undesirable freshwater or salt-water fish, such as perch or wrasse, which, after being caught by an angler seeking more valuable fish, is propelled violently through the air with a brisk arm movement.
Fork	The point at which an unproductive river divides into two unpromising streams.

G

Gadget	Bright, alluring object with an inconspicuous price tag placed in a prominent position in a bait and tackle shop or moved slowly under the nose of a browsing angler.
Game Fish	Any fish that puts up as much of a fight when being caught as the angler's spouse did prior to his departure.
Gravel Bar	*1.* Mound or bank of pebbles found in streams and rivers. *2.* Candy product that has melted and resolidified in the bottom of a pack or duffle bag.
Grilse	Young salmon returning from salt-water to spawn. Salmon are the moodiest and most unpredictable of fish, and thus are very hard to generalise about, but very broadly speaking, the best time to fish for salmon is an hour or two before you arrive at a stream or shortly after you leave. As

Hats

WESSEX

ALPINE

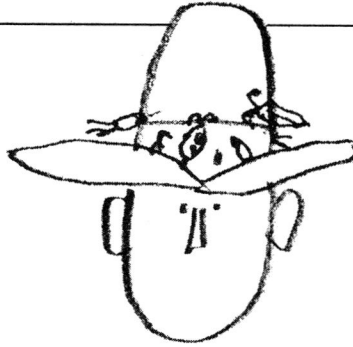

TRUE GRIT

NIGHT

SCOTCH SALMON

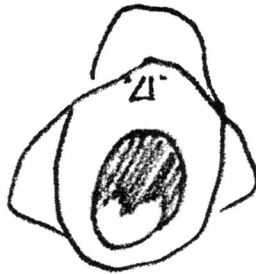

WAILER

HENLEY

ICE

PARTY BOAT

DRY FLY

WET FLY

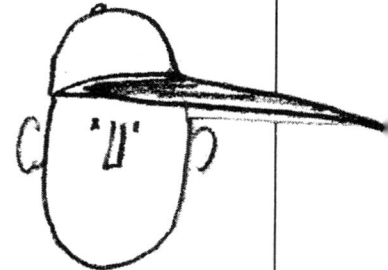

SPORT

far as lures go, almost any fly not in your fly book is a pretty good bet, though you might have had some luck with the one that got hooked in your pocket. There's a good deal of debate about casting methods, but whether you let the fly drift by the fish so gently that it doesn't notice it or tweak it so that it scares it, the results are about equal. As for the likeliest places to find salmon, the best spot to be is on the other side of the river, 10 miles upstream, or back at that pool you passed 3 hours ago.

Guide

1. One of a series of ring-shaped metal loops through which the line passes on a fishing rod. Typically, there is one just above the butt, several along the midsection, and one at the tip. *2.* Professional fishing assistant. Fishermen should be aware that guides planning the loading of the boat, the number and type of meals to be served, and the degree of service to be provided, divide the angler into three basic sections: the butt, the midsection, and the tip.

H

Habitat

Place where a particular species of fish was last week.

Haddock

Very important commercial fish, related to cod, found in ocean waters. It has long been a favourite of preparers of institutional food since its somewhat gluey flesh can be easily formed into sticks, cakes, lumps, slabs, nuggets, and balls, and will generally not disintegrate when cooked if coated with a protective batter made of equal parts plaster of Paris and blackboard chalk and fried for no longer than 3 hours at 1,100° F.

Hat

Anything on the head of a fisherman that does not bite or fly away when struck sharply with the hand.

Ice Fishing

Hatch	Simultaneous appearance on a single stretch of stream of a large number of insects of the same species which causes fish to rise and feed voraciously and makes them somewhat susceptible to capture. It is impossible to predict exactly when a hatch will take place, but generally speaking, they occur on Mondays, during unusually heavy rains, or on the Wednesday immediately preceding or immediately following a bank holiday weekend.
Hook	Irritating but highly reliable device used to quickly locate the position of one's thumb at the bottom of a tackle box.
Hot Spot	*1.* Place on any given stream or lake, usually known only to locals, where fish can be found. *2.* Place in the centre of the palm of the right hand of locals where money may be placed to help find *1*.

I

Ice Fishing	Winter fishing method in which anglers use a variety of specialised equipment to catch colds.
Inchworm	Tiny moth larva favoured as food by trout and as bait by trout fishermen, who, from force of deep-rooted habits, invariably refer to them as foot-and-a-halfworms.
Indoor Casting	The angler anxious to improve his casting skills can profitably practise indoors. This is an ideal exercise, since it does away with the major inconveniences of fishing, such as cold water, bugs, tedious and costly trips to remote places, and the troublesome fish itself, while preserving the display of delicate skill that is the essence of fine fishing

Indoor Casting

technique. Seated by the pool with a cool drink or reclining on a comfortable "casting couch" in his own living room, the home fisherman can, depending on his level of experience, use simple tackle and subtle casts to change television channels, turn on a light, snatch a detective novel off a distant shelf, procure a snack from the kitchen, or restrain an unruly child. And for those who miss the realism of stalking a quarry, the appropriate gear may be used to have a little sport with the Avon lady, walk a pet in bad weather without leaving the house, or obtain produce from a neighbour's garden.

In-flight Testing	As a free service to anglers embarking on fishing trips, all major airlines subject fishing rods, tackle boxes, and other gear to an exhaustive series of rigorous trials intended to spot any flaws in design or packaging. There is no need to make special arrangements for this procedure—just hand your angling paraphernalia to the attendant at the check-in counter. It will be immediately placed on a high-speed conveyor belt to begin its carefully planned ordeal. The exact testing process is a closely guarded industry secret, but based on an examination of samples of fishing outfits that have undergone this thorough shakedown, it involves the application of every form of compression, concussion, corrosion, vibration, and perforation known to modern science, and if your rig emerges in usable condition, you can take justifiable pride in the knowledge that you are the owner of rugged, reliable, and absolutely indestructible fishing equipment.
Insect Repellent	One of a number of "joke" items available in bait and tackle shops.

Knot (Basic Procedure)

STEP I

STEP II

STEP III

STEP IV

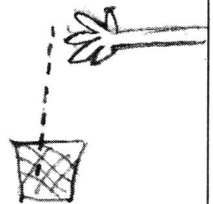

J

Jack-knife	Indispensable cutting tool generally found in the pocket of a different jacket, beneath the front seat of the car, or under the roll of screening on the table in the garage.
Jig	Crude but effective artificial lure made up of a metal head and some form of dressing designed not to imitate a particular food favoured by fish, but to attract their attention through its motions in the water. Jigs are the simplest and most ancient of fishing lures, and in fact, the oldest known evidence of angling is a carved elk horn jig mounted on a bone hook found deeply embedded in a petrified log near the remains of a remarkably well-preserved, 14,000 year-old Swiss lake village. Interestingly enough, next to it were the sharply broken remains of a rough-hewn oak pole and a small woven reed basket containing the bones of three tiny, long-extinct minnows.

K

Kapok	*1.* Silky fibres used as stuffing in boat cushions. *2.* Promising backfiring sound made by outboard motor after 30 pulls of the starting cord.
Kit	Prepackaged, partly finished, unassembled object, such as a fishing rod, which comes in a box containing all but three of the required parts; a list of 220-volt power tools essential for its completion; and pages 1-12 and 24-32 of the Dutch language instructions.
Knot	A tangle with a name.

Lake (The Fishing Cycle Explained)

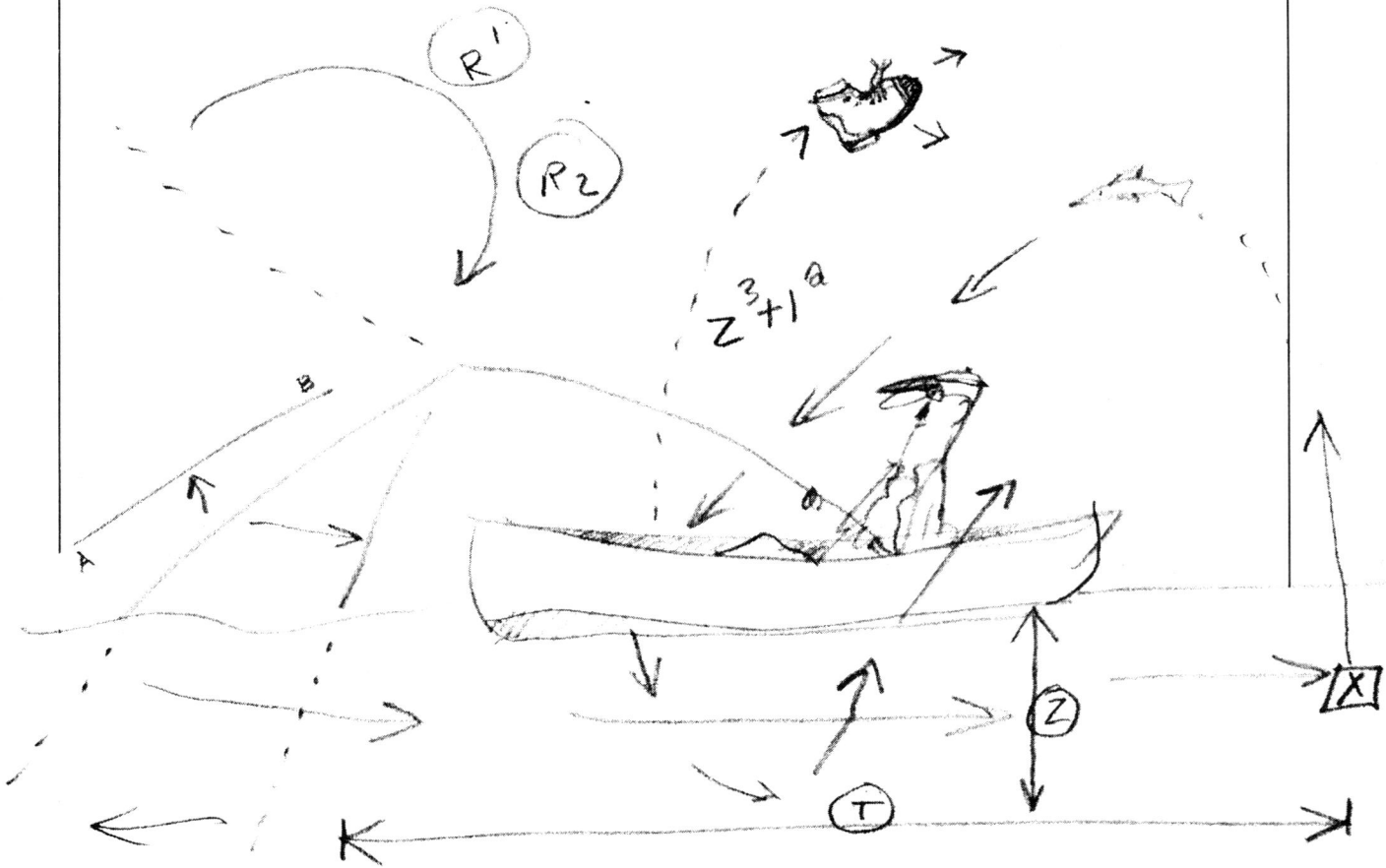

R¹

R₂

$Z^3 + 1^a$

Z

T

X

L

Lake	Ecologists classify lakes as being oligotrophic (low in nourishment) or eutrophic (high in nourishment), and while terms such as these are of some interest to anglers eager to learn about the life cycles of various fish species, most fishermen prefer to know whether a given lake is autocatastrophic (approachable only by deeply rutted dirt roads); peptobismolic (unfit to drink); psychomotorphobic (frequented by maniacs in overpowered speedboats); or photosoporific (possessing the sort of scenic beauty that causes anglers to take boring holiday snaps of it.
Leader	Short length of nylon or wire that connects a snagged lure to a tangled line.
Leadhead	*1.* Slang term for a particular type of metal jig. *2.* Unpleasant cranial condition suffered in the morning hours by dedicated anglers who, in the interests of better understanding their quarry, spent the previous evening attempting to imitate fishes' widely noted ability to process large amounts of liquid.
Leech	*1.* Blood-sucking parasitic worm that attaches itself with a pair of suckers to the legs of wading fishermen. The bite is not really all that serious, and since the leech introduces a small amount of an irritating anticoagulant into the wound, the most sensible thing to do is to leave the leech in place until it drops off of its own accord, at which point it will have withdrawn the itch-producing substance. *2.* Aaaaaaaaaaaaaaaaaaaaaaaaaaaaaaaaaaaaaaaaaaaaagh.
License	Permit issued upon payment of a modest fee that allows fishermen to lose lures in a specified area.

Lie	*1.* A place in a stream, river, or lake where fish lurk. *2.* Any simple declarative statement made by an angler about the location of such a place; or the number, size, and type of fish observed there; or the circumstances under which one or more of them escaped capture.
Limit	Maximum number of a particular fish that an angler can take in a day. This number varies from place to place and species to species, but like the speed of light, it is a largely theoretical restriction with little practical application.
Line	Length of filament stretched between two fishing rods and joined at its midpoint by a pair of linked hooks.
Loch Ness	Scottish lake with potentially very dramatic, though highly specialised fishing. In the way of gear, most anglers select an 8-ton crane with a mile of $\frac{5}{8}$ inch stainless steel cable, with a No. 9 cargo hook baited with a well-stocked tea trolley or several whole Stiltons. Nothing has been caught yet, but there are some very entertaining stories.
Lodge	Overnight accommodation in fishing area. The term is sometimes used rather loosely, but in most areas, to be classified as a lodge rather than a motel, an establishment must meet certain criteria: it must possess 90 per cent of the *National Geographics* published between 1955 and 1970; it must have a black-and-white television set manufactured prior to 1965; it must have no more than six items on its menu at any one time—and one of them must be corned beef hash; it must have a sign reading "We Aim To Please, You Aim Too, Please" prominently posted in the downstairs men's room and a copy of "The Angler's Prayer" displayed in the main hallway; there must be at least six blue spruces, forty whitewashed boulders, and one

large deaf dog on the grounds; the operation of any plumbing fixture in any portion of the building must be clearly audible to every occupant of the building; and the proprietor or proprietress must be able to expound at length, without notes, on all the major theories of climatological change, including the greenhouse effect, the sunspot cycle, the melting of the ice caps, and the effect of rocket-launchings on rain.

Logjam   *1.* Obstruction in a river caused by an accumulation of tangled tree trunks. *2.* Unpleasant sticky substance found on tree trunks used as seats at campsite breakfasts.

Luck   One of the most frustrating circumstances in fishing occurs when two anglers in the same boat experience dramatically different results: one catches fish methodically, the other gets nary a nibble. Obviously, the "unlucky" angler is doing something wrong, and if this happens to you, you should take a moment to question your technique. First, examine your posture. When your companion casts, are you reaching forward to nudge him with your elbow or inconspicuously shifting your weight back and forth to impart a disorienting rocking motion to the boat? Second, are you paying enough attention to the lure? Have you surreptitiously daubed your fellow angler's fly or plug with motor oil or insect repellent or some smelly rod glue? And what about the retrieve? Have you slipped a small amount of honey into the moving parts of his reel mechanism and imparted kinks and twists in any line he has stripped off onto the bottom of the boat? And when you assist your colleague in netting fish, do you use the backhand flub and the underwater hook snap? Well, we could go on, but remember, in angling, skill always wins out over luck.

Lure	Anything used to attract fish. There are basically two kinds: those fishermen swear by, and those they swear at.

M

Maintenance	It only takes a few moments at the end of each fishing season to ensure that your gear will be in proper condition for use the following year. Of course, each individual fisherman will have his own maintenance programme, but we recommend the basic procedures listed here, which have been perfected over many years by countless anglers: *(a)* Put reels in the pockets of an old army jacket or overcoat—do not remove line. *(b)* Disassemble fishing rod, slip into a partly opened umbrella, and lean in a dark corner. *(c)* Place an open can of lubricating oil in tackle boxes and store them upside down on the floor or a high shelf. *(d)* Roll waders, vest, and other pieces of clothing into a tight ball and throw into the back of the cupboard. *(e)* Drop any loose hooks and lures into your landing net and store under the kitchen sink. *(f)* Toss tools, gadgets, and leftover fly dope into creel and wedge behind couch.
Map	Handy, schematic representation of all the various roads in a given area that you are not currently on.
Matching the Hatch	*1.* The art of creating, out of bits of feather and hair, convincing replicas of insects being eaten by fish for use as bait. *2.* The far more demanding practice of trussing up

and immobilising the actual insect itself with tiny handcuffs, shackles, and leg irons prior to attaching it to a hook. This exacting craft, which may entail, before each cast, two hours or more of patient labour to turn, say, a single millipede into a little chain gang, is favoured by ultratraditional anglers, but has been opposed for years by the Society for the Prevention of Cruelty to Insects. However, due to that organisation's very small membership—34 at last count—and the fact that all but six of them are currently incarcerated in institutions for the disturbed, its protests have had little practical effect.

Measurement of Fish	There are a number of different methods of determining the overall length in inches of freshwater fish, and anglers are free to choose the one that suits them best. The most common are: the distance from the centre of the tail of the fish, while still hooked, to the tip of the fishing rod; the distance from the tip of the snout to the end of the handle of the landing net; the distance from the front of the gill of a fish held in the hand to the inside edge of the holder's elbow; four times the angler's shoe size or five times his hat size; and the temperature in degrees Fahrenheit, divided by 2 (summer) or multiplied by 2 (winter).
Minnow	*1.* Informal term for any very small fish. *2.* Embryonic stage of a large fib.
Moray	Variety of eel so favoured by Italian chefs that it is the subject of a popular song: "When an eel bites your heel with its jaws made of steel, that's a Moray."
Myth	Technical term for a basic piece of factual angling information contained in one fishing book when referred to by the author of another fishing book.

Myth (No. 26: "There Are No Sharks in Inland Waters.")

Net (1., 2., 3.)

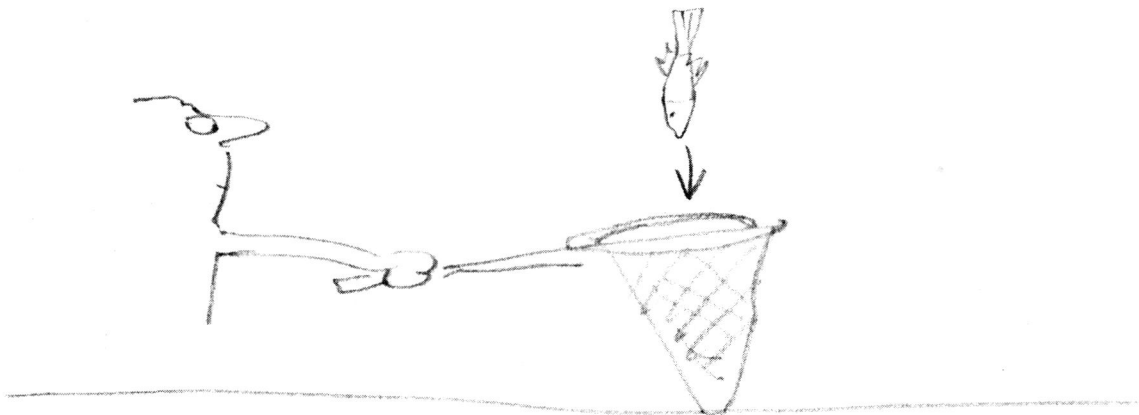

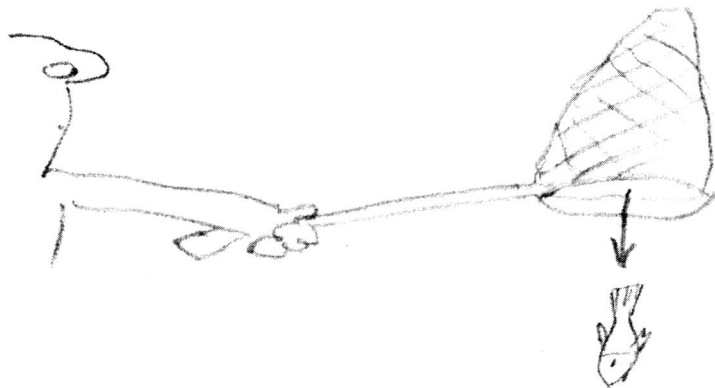

N

Natural	Type of organic bait rejected by a finicky fish because it is too large or too small, or because it has the wrong shape, bears the wrong colouration, or makes the wrong motions in the water. *See* ARTIFICIAL.
Net	*1. n.* Woven mesh bag attached to a circular wood or metal frame on which a handle is mounted used to remove hooked fish from the water. *2. v.* To land or capture a fish, as in, "I netted 15 one-pound trout." *3. adj.* The final or actual amount or weight following adjustments for loss and reductions due to overstatement, as in, "Well, if we're talking net here, maybe it was one 15-ounce trout."
Nymph	*1.* The underwater stage of certain insects eaten by fish or any fly designed to imitate it. *2.* The words "Net!", "Now!", "No!", "Nuts!", and "Ninny!" as spoken to a companion by a fly fisherman holding loops of fly line in his mouth.

O

Oar	Clumsy wooden implement used to moisten boat occupants.
Ob	Siberian river familiar to anglers who have spent a rainy week in a cabin with a 47-card poker deck, the March, 1957, issue of *Illustrated*, and 20 crossword puzzle books.
Opening Day	The first day of the angling season in some parts of the country is 1 April, which is often referred to by the name

Party Boat

April Fisherman's Day or a similar term honouring the sport, and even non-fishermen get into the spirit of this popular national pastime by practising harmless deceptions on one another.

P

Panfish	Anything removed from the water that will fit into a frying pan and does not melt, smoulder, or give off sparks when cooked.
Party Boat	Large salt-water fishing craft that carries a sizable number of fishermen, each of whom is charged a fixed fee for the outing, which usually includes bait and sometimes the use of fishing tackle as well. Party boats are almost always crowded, and since the individual who catches the largest fish generally wins a pool made up of contributions by all on board, tempers can quickly flare in close quarters when lines become tangled—as they inevitably do—or when a nearby angler's clumsiness causes a fish to be lost. For this reason, adherence to a few simple forms of shipboard etiquette is very important. For example, an individual should always be tapped lightly from behind on the right shoulder before being struck on the nose or chin; if bait has been handled recently, hands should be thoroughly washed before being placed around the neck of a fellow fisherman whom one wishes to throttle; an angler who fails to respond to a slow count of 10 is presumed to have given up his fishing position along the rail; and under no circumstances should an individual be knocked overboard while the fish are biting.

Plastic Lures

Pattern	Characteristic size, shape, colour, and texture of an artificial fly. Anglers achieve a specific look by tying various kinds of bird feathers and animal hair onto the shank of a hook. Although there are dozens of patterns, most anglers create and carry two basic kinds of designs: "dummies"—or "foolers"—which are carefully crafted out of substances and colours with a proven ability to alarm and annoy fish, are prominently displayed on a hat brim or waistcoat pocket, and are generously lent to fellow anglers for copying or immediate use; and "actuals," highly effective stream-tested designs that are hidden in a small box or tucked away in an inside pocket.
Perch	*1.* Spiny coarse fish found in many aquatic habitats. *2.* Standing place, such as a slippery bank, wet rock, or rickety platform, from which an angler was fishing for perch shortly before he unexpectedly entered the perch's habitat.
Plastic Lures	Lifelike and effective plastic imitations of worms, frogs, squid, and other favourite fish foods are widely used, but many anglers are unaware of other equally convincing and useful stream-side accoutrements, including the unbelievably realistic 12-foot Vinylmouth, a snake which—when placed in a highly visible spot—can reliably clear a mile or two of stream of competing anglers in less than a minute, and the radio-controlled Mesmerisers, a pair of totally believable rubber decoys (either the 19-inch rainbow trout or the 22-inch mirror carp) that are capable of executing up to 40 different pre-programmed teasing manoeuvres designed to keep dozens of potentially bothersome fellow fishermen glued to a worthless downstream pool or a barren stretch of lake shore for hours on end.

Playing	*1.* Series of rod, reel, and line motions used by the angler to tire a hooked fish and eventually drive it—in a state of exhaustion—into a net. *2.* Series of tantalising nibbles, tail flips, and short jumps used by fish to madden a hooked angler and eventually drive him into a state of mind that will result in someone coming after him with a net.
Plug	Plastic or wooden lure designed to imitate various species of bait fish. Typically, they produce a popping noise or a provocative motion as they are pulled through the water that is intended either to attract the attention of fish or to annoy them into striking. In the latter category of effects, the most elaborate plug is the costly, but lethal Raspberry, which uses a small waterproof cassette recorder and an underwater loudspeaker to make a variety of hisses, boos, hoots, and catcalls, interspersed with pre-recorded gibes like, "Hey, minnow-breath, are you going to bite me or just sit there like a pile of silt and make bubbles?" and, "You know why fish live in the water? Because they're all wet! Har, har, har."
Poaching	*1.* Stealing fish. *2.* Method of disposing of the evidence by boiling it into an unrecognisable sludge.
Pocket Water	*1.* Stream surface condition characterised by pools of water which form downstream from large rocks. *2.* Small impoundment of water often encountered by anglers when fishing for keys, change, folding money, or matches.
Pollan	See VENDACE.
Pond	Large volume of water surrounding a snapping turtle.
Portage	The shortest distance between two hernias.

Prawn	Food favoured both by fish and by fishermen. Other shared affinities include getting covered with slime, wriggling in the mud, and spending long periods in cold water.
Prize Fish	Any fish that weighs more than the gear used to catch it.
Propeller	Motor-operated device used on powered fishing craft to take up very large amounts of fishing line at an extremely high rate of speed.
Pupa	The intermediate stage in the development of an insect, which occurs after it is completely revolting and before it is thoroughly annoying.
Put Down	To scare a fish. Although fish see things somewhat differently from the way humans do, most have quite good vision, and unexpected or unfamiliar shapes can quickly scare them off. Anglers eager to improve their chances of getting close to particularly skittish species, like wild trout, have gone so far as to invest in modern dance lessons to be able to imitate saplings or shrubbery, but a far simpler method is to acquire one of the new, amazingly realistic rubber fish suits with lifelike scales and fin-shaped waders. Another excellent choice, if cost is no object, is the Motor Maggot, a natural-looking 14-foot mechanical caterpillar, which provides comfortable fishing positions for two anglers whose rods project through apertures in the "head," closely mimicking an insect's antennae. It is available in a choice of colourations to blend with local flora, and thanks to a unique muffling system which makes exhaust noises sound like the cry of a barn owl (albeit an unusually deep-voiced specimen), it can approach right to the stream edge without scaring a nervy trout.

Prize Fish

Records

Q

Quill
Type of feather material attached to a hook shank to imitate the look of an insect's segmented body. How it is that, say, a trout, which has extremely acute eyesight, can mistake a crude clump of duck feathers and deer fur for some insect it sees every day is a complete mystery, but it certainly undermines the concept of fish as "brain food."

R

Records
The names of current holders of records for game fish are widely published in fishing journals, but individuals who have set new marks in other categories of angling often go unsung. This seems a bit unfair, and it is hoped that this short list will go a long way towards rectifying the more serious omissions:

TYRE: 1965, Grafham Water, 51½ pounds, 35 inches in diameter, Mr. Edward T. Rutherford.

BOOT: 1971, Itchen Abbas, 7¼ pounds, size 11, Mr. Vincent Castelli.

OBSTRUCTION: 1958, Southampton Water, elm root, 36 pounds, 22 inches, Mr. Joseph Ward.

JETSAM, FRESHWATER: 1976, River Dee, electric toaster, 11 pounds, 28 inches (to tip of electric cord), Mrs. Alice Leighton.

JETSAM, SALT-WATER: 1960, Rye Harbour, golf club bag with clubs, 38¼ pounds, 44 inches, Mr. Thomas P. Landsdowne.

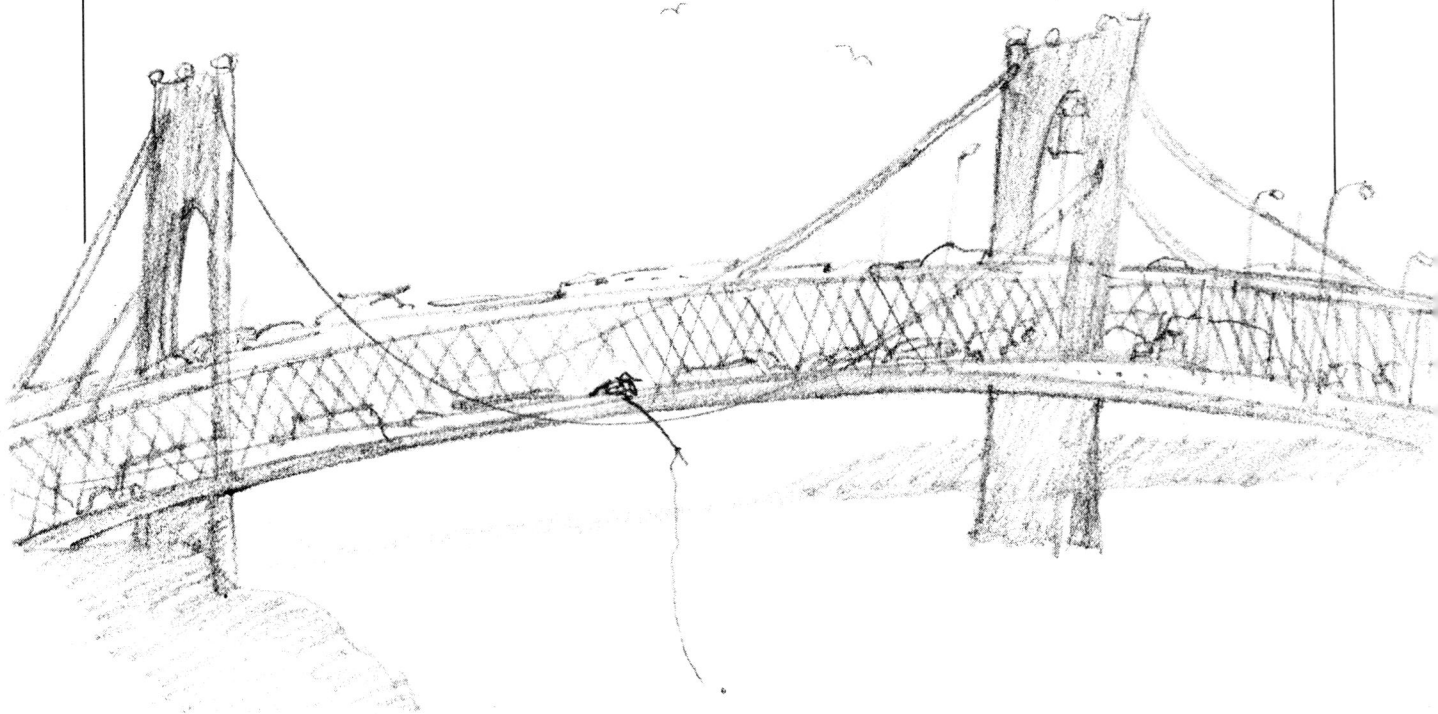

River

Reel	Cylindrical device attached near the end of a fishing rod for winding up or letting out line. There are several different types and sizes designed for a wide range of fishing situations, but they all offer the angler the option of two basic settings: "wheeeeee," in which at the slightest pull, the line is paid out in a series of erratic loops at very high speed; and "fonk," in which the reel spontaneously stops revolving with a sharp metallic sound, instantly dividing the line into two sections of unequal length.
Regionalisms	A source of both charm and confusion in the world of angling is the prevalence of local terms. For example, the ubiquitous water-skier found in temperate zones in summer months is known to fishermen variously as the lake nerd, water turkey, harbour dolt, pond prat, surf oaf, or river wally, and an angler fishing close by is referred to in different parts of the country as a blockhead, fathead, meathead, lunkhead, blunderhead, dunderpate, numbskull, knucklehead, lamebrain or nitwit. It can all be a little bewildering, but it does add colour to the sport!
Reservoir	A flood named after a politician.
River	Any stretch of moving water large enough to be crossed by a bridge from which fishing is prohibited.
Rod	Flexible, tapered stick that is the basic tool of angling. Many fishermen find rods of even average length to be awkward to carry, but they can easily be shortened to a more convenient size by removing the top few inches with an ordinary car door or boot lid.
Rod Belt	*1.* A belt with a cup where the butt of a surf rod may be rested. *2.* Brief drink of a stimulating beverage.

Rules of Thumb ("Don't Let Anyone Hold Your Fish.")

Rod Casting	The discouraged angler who has decided to bid farewell to his hobby should do so with the same style and attention to form that he displayed while he practised it. Stand on a stream bank, lake shore, pier, or beach, with feet placed comfortably apart, and grasp the fishing rod by the cork handle. Select a sinker large enough to overcome the natural buoyancy of the rod, attach it securely to the line, then slip the hook over the lowest guide, tightening and locking the reel so that the rod has a slight bend. Hold the rod straight out in front of you, then smoothly raise your arm over your head until the rod is almost parallel with the ground behind you. Make any brief remarks you wish, then with a fast, overhead whipping motion of the arm and elbow, propel the rod forward and slightly up. Just before release, give a quick snap of the wrist, and as the rod strikes the water, "dust" your hands with a few brisk sliding motions of one palm across the other.
Roe	Fish eggs. Only those from sturgeon are properly called caviare. Other fish from which roe is taken, and the names under which it is usually sold, are salmon (caviare), mullet (caviare), lumpfish (caviare), and whitefish (caviare).
Rules of Thumb	Given the enormous number of different fishing techniques, very few maxims have universal application, but the handful that do are worth committing to memory: (*a*) Never drink beer in waders. (*b*) Never fish with a vicar. (*c*) Don't tell jokes in canoes. (*d*) On ocean-going party boats, always fish to windward. (*e*) On camping trips, always bring books with large, soft pages. (*f*) Don't take advice from people with missing fingers.

Salmon (Fishing the Run)

S

Salmon	During those rare times when these magnificent fish are biting, they provide some of the most sensational sport in angling, and even during the many long days when they aren't, they still offer some diversion to occupy patient anglers in fishing hotels, since they are an incredibly rich source of obscure Scrabble words, including kype, redd, parr, vomer, milt, smolt, grilse, and kelt.
Scales	*1.* Annoying things on fish. *2.* Annoying things on docks.
Scotland	Peculiar land that is the birthplace of golf and sport salmon fishing, a fact which may explain why it is also the birthplace of whisky.
Scrod	*1. n.* Commercial name for young cod or haddock fillets. *2. v.* Having been unfairly dealt with in a business transaction at a bait-and-tackle shop.
Sea Food	Anglers who live near the shore can be assured of a ready supply of delicious and healthful fish products with a minimum of trouble and expense if they keep their eyes open and use a little common sense. There's no need for costly rods and reels or budget-busting boat charters, because British Telecom in most areas has listed the likeliest spots where fish can be "taken" in a handy guide printed on yellow paper. You'll be in luck any time from about nine in the morning until five in the evening (except Sunday), and the only "lure" you'll need is the old reliable quids or fivers, though if you insist on a little sport, you can always try a rubber cheque or a plastic credit card first.

Sea Trout

Extremely sporting and hard-fighting migratory cousin of the brown trout which is usually taken with fly tackle. Angling for these exceptionally game fish is done primarily at night, and since the business of selecting and attaching flies must be done in the dark, the most popular sea trout lures are the Muddle, the Bollix, the Full Bobble, the Fumbleduff, the Yorkshire Gowk, and the Royal Fiasco.

Seaweed

Form of marine life sought after by vegetarian sportsmen. With the exception of the giant kelp, most species of algae don't put up much of a fight, but for the angler on an ocean-going "scumboat," the deceptively offhand remark from a crewman that "it looks like there's some algae up ahead," the sodden gurgle as the large hooks bite into the shimmering green mass, and the arm-numbing struggle to boat the bubbling glob of treacherous goo are the stuff of oft-told tales whenever two or three "weed-eaters" gather for a bowl of sea lettuce and some clam juice and swap stories of man against mush and "the ton that got away."

Sinker

1. Lead weight attached to the end of a length of fishing line to facilitate the speedy disposal of unwanted lures. *2.* Wooden boat kept by Irish hoteliers for the benefit of the fishing guest not using the hotel ghillie.

Slip

1. Mooring system in which a boat is tied alongside one of a series of floating piers projecting at right angles from a dock. *2.* Common method of entering such a boat.

Smelt

1. n. Small, oily fish that occurs in large schools in both fresh and salt water. *2. v.* Discovered or located through the use of the olfactory sense. The best method of finding misplaced fish.

Spearfishing

Sneck, Garrison	(1857-1909) Noted angler and author of *The Superiority of Grey-Winged Fly Patterns in Trout Streams.*
Snell, Francis	(1849-1909) Noted angler and author of *An Exhaustive Comparison of Wet Streamers with Unsatisfactory Alternatives, Particularly the Grey- and Buff-Winged Flies.*
Snood, Herman	(1853-1909) Noted angler and author of *The Outstanding Qualities of the Buff-Winged Fly Conclusively Demonstrated Over Wet Streamers and All Grey-Winged Patterns.*
Snook, Gideon	(1855-1934) Noted angler and author of *An Absolute Refutation of Previous Misguided Theories on Flies and Streamers Propounded by Witless Amateurs.* It was Snook who arranged the ill-fated fishing party of April, 1909, for the purpose, as he wrote to a friend in the celebrated letter that played so large a part at his trial, "of finally resolving this question of which lure is preferred by the trout—I suppose I can endure the company of these three button-brains for one day if it means settling this matter once and for all". His later books include *Fly-Tying with Wrists Restrained, Practice-Casting in Confined Spaces,* and *A Study of Insects of Interest to Anglers in the Vicinity of Wormwood Scrubs.*
Solitude	State of being closer to nature than to the nearest flush toilet.
Spanish Mackerel	Medium-sized, Atlantic game fish found as far south as Brazil. They are typically caught by sport fishermen using a hook tied with a strip of silk and baited with a dab of pommade, and by commercial fishermen using castanets.
Spearfishing	Angling method that combines the sports of diving, fishing, and, if sharks are sighted, Olympic swimming.

Species	Although there are thousands of different marine animals in the world's oceans, lakes, rivers, and estuaries, they can all be placed into one of ten broad scientific categories: Toothy/Nasty; Scaly/Slimy; Lumpy/Smelly; Angry/Hungry; Ugly/Puffy; Mushy/Stinky; Slinky/Creepy; Spiky/Nubby; Ghastly/Spiny; and Simply/Unbelievable.
Spin Casting	Angling method employing a fishing rod whose reel is completely enclosed in a cone-shaped housing. Release of the line during the cast is accomplished with a handy push-button operated by the thumb. The relatively trouble-free operation of this simple, automatic rig often makes it an object of vocal disparagement by anglers using more traditional gear, but aficionados of spin-casting outfits take such chaffing and light-hearted abuse in stride and patiently bide their time, for they find that its almost foolproof operation leaves their minds free to concentrate on formulating complex, elegant insults, such as, "Sir, if it is your intention to cover this stream with a web, might I suggest that you hire spiders?" to which the preoccupied fly caster or bait caster, his hands fumbling with five feet of knotted fishing line, is usually only capable of replying, with a muttered "Sod off," and an ineffectual vulgar gesture.
Spinner	Popular fishing lure commonly used by spin-casters which typically consists of a rusted, pitted, dented, or tarnished blade-shaped piece of metal attached to a broken swivel or a bent shaft by a jammed locking device.
Spool	Smooth, hard container from which—during daylight hours when fish are biting—there periodically hatches the full-blown snarl or tangle.

Spin Casting
(The Drawbacks of the Fly Rod)

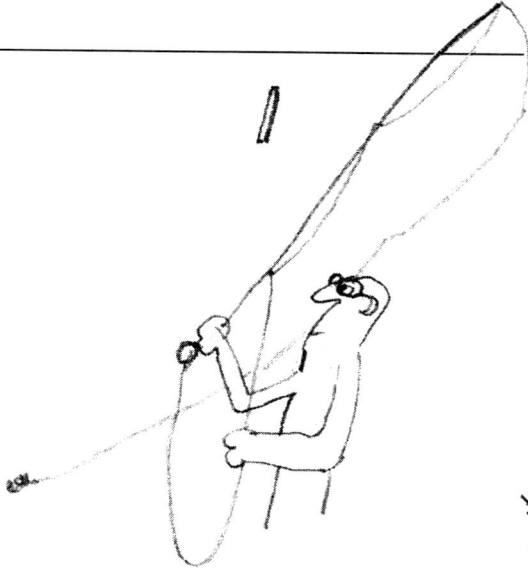

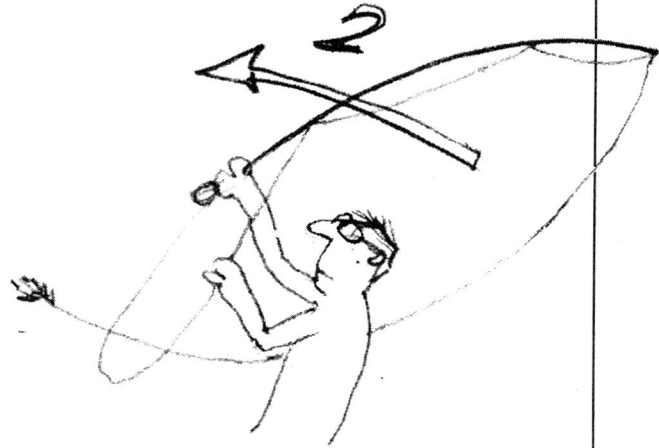

Surf Fishing

Spoon	Widely used metal fishing lure. It is particularly popular among anglers who intend to make a meal of their catch since if it is unsuccessful in attracting fish, it may be employed to consume the contents of a can of Ambrosia Creamed Rice.
Squid	*1.* Any of a variety of marine cephalopods often used as bait for salt-water fish. *2.* The sound made when one inadvertently steps on a marine cephalopod left on deck.
Still Fishing	Fishing technique usually characterised by a long stretch of time spent by the angler lying quietly, followed by a shorter period during which he lies noisily.
Stream	The means by which fish pass from a place where they were biting a week before you came to a place where they will be biting a week after you leave.
Strike	The moment when, with a quick rolling or lunging motion, an unseen quarry suddenly takes the hook of an angler fishing the spot you left 10 minutes ago.
Surf fishing	Angling for shore-feeding fish, usually from a beach. Although this is generally done in early morning and early evening hours, surf fishermen must be alert to the presence of swimmers—large, semiaquatic creatures who are normally quite playful, but can become extremely ill-tempered when hooked.

T

Tackle	Any fishing gear which, when left on the ground or the bottom of a boat, is capable of suddenly halting an angler's forward progress towards a desired goal.

Tarpon (Trophy Size)

Tag

Identifying label affixed to a member of a given species as an aid in determining its migratory patterns and any significant changes in size, form, and habits. A greater knowledge of the mysterious world of fishing has been gained from a study of individuals marked in this manner, whose sometimes incredible wanderings have been documented with the assistance of a world-wide network of co-operative amateurs. Just to cite one example of their work, a mature stockbroker labelled in 1981 in Leatherhead, with an unobtrusive aluminium badge clipped to his favourite hat was found to have travelled in a single year to Rutland, Craigellachie, Orkney, Shetland, Cromarty, Faroes and South Uist. When finally reencountered in a bar in Glasgow, it turned out that he had not caught a single fish during this entire period. Still, although he had lost 27 pounds, and had a seriously depleted bank account, his eyes were bright, his pulse was strong, and he was about to embark on a fishing expedition to Alaska. Perhaps one day through a study of cases like these we will have some clue to the extraordinary impulse that triggers these truly heroic journeys!

Tarpon

In the opinion of many salt-water anglers, this primitive Atlantic species is the ideal game fish. It is only found in places that cost a good deal of money to get to. It is often accompanied by sharks. It is nearly impossible to hook, and once hooked, equally difficult to boat. When boated, it often has enough fight left to injure the fisherman or damage the boat. It has hundreds of large sharp scales, and its flesh is bony and inedible. All it lacks are a foul odour, poisonous spines, and the teeth of a piranha, but presumably crossbreeding will one day rectify these omissions.

Test

Taxidermy	Preparation for display of prize fish. Actually, the term is a misnomer, since fish are almost never stuffed—it simply isn't practical. Instead, a mould is made of the body, and a durable synthetic duplicate is produced from it, and this duplicate is then hand-painted to resemble the original fish. There are several materials available from which these reproductions may be made, but by far the most popular is a type of super-stretchable rubber used in golf-ball windings. This remarkable substance not only provides an ideal surface for delicate portrayal of skin colouration and scale shape, but also permits models made from it to be mounted on a spring-loaded expansion backing which can increase their size by up to 700 per cent.
Tent	Cumbersome device composed of fabric and tubing used by fishermen camping in the woods to collect specimens of local insects.
Test	Fishing line is clearly marked with its test—that is, the amount of linear force, in pounds, that can be exerted on it before it breaks. But an angler has enough to do playing the wily adversary at the end of his line without trying to mentally estimate linear stresses, so here is a brief table of the strains exerted by the most commonly hooked casting targets:

HAT: 1 lb.   CAR AERIAL: 15 lb.
PICNIC LUNCH: 3 lb.   VINE OR BUSH: 30 lb.
SHOE (loose): 4 lb.   SAPLING: 40 lb.
TWIG: 10 lb.   SHOE (on foot): 55 lb.
BOX OF LURES: 12 lb.   BACK OF JACKET: 75 lb.

Thumb	Fingerlike appendages of limited mobility found at the ends of the hands. Interestingly, most anglers and fly-tyers have ten of them.

Tippling	Method of night fishing in which each cast is followed by a short pull or tug on a bottle held in the free hand. This can lead to erratic casting, but it has the advantage that after a fairly brief period, fish are caught two at a time.
Traditional	Any fishing technique that was conclusively proven to be impractical, ineffective, needlessly costly, or impossibly time-consuming prior to the year 1900. See UNSPORTING.
Troll	*1. v.* To trail a bait behind a moving boat. *2. n.* Legendary creature thought to dwell in secluded spots in rivers from which it lures people to their doom.
Trout	*1.* Greatly valued game fish of the Salmonidae family. *2.* Legendary creature thought to dwell in secluded spots in rivers from which it lures people to their doom.
Tuna	There are a number of varieties of this tasty game fish, but from the sport fisherman's viewpoint, the most important is the giant bluefin, examples of which have been known to exceed 1,000 pounds. It's hard to imagine a fish of that size, but perhaps a few comparisons will help: a half-ton bluefin would be equal to 2,345 sandwiches, 880 gallons of tuna-noodle casserole (standard recipe), or a bowl of tuna fish dip 28 feet in diameter and 7 feet deep!
Turbot	Delicate flatfish, esteemed by gourmets. It is a mainstay of French cuisine, which, regrettably, features other far less appealing types of fish. In fact, French seafood comes in four basic types: *1.* A tiny piece of something quite nice in some kind of sauce; *2.* A lot of very odd things in a sort of stew; *3.* A slab of something really rather nasty in some more of that sauce, only thicker; and *4.* A large metal tray holding exhibits from the local marine museum.

Troll

Utility Boat

U

Unsporting	Any fishing technique that has as its object the capture of fish rather than the accumulation of fishing equipment.
Utility Boat	All-purpose boat used by many fishermen. More specialised fishing boats have been around for over a century, but the appearance in the last two decades of highly refined fishing craft, like the elaborate sea-going vessels equipped with electronic gear that are little more than machines for catching fish, has begun to trouble many anglers. It's a matter of personal taste where the line between angling and fish murder lies, but certainly the recently introduced LCT (Landing Craft, Trout) with its insect radar and hydraulic dry- and wet-fly catapults is awfully close to it, and the new and deadly sonar-equipped salmon submarines are well over it.

V

Vendace	Freshwater herring or whitefish often confused with the Powan, Gwyniad and Skelly. Only one has ever been caught.

W

Wading	The most common means through which a dry-fly fisherman is transformed into a wet-fly fisherman.
Wading Staff	Although there are specially designed collapsible metal

poles to help anglers keep their balance as they pick their way along slippery rocks in freezing, fast-moving streams, many fishermen prefer to use an old golf club, ski pole, or the handle of a hoe, which not only serve as cheap and reliable substitutes, but also provide a comforting reminder of the constant availability of alternative pastimes.

Wahoo	*1.* Salt-water game fish in the mackerel family. *2.* Remark made by an angler who inadvertently sits on a treble-hooked salt-water fishing lure.
Waistcoat	Ideal freshwater fishing garment. In its pockets, or pinned or clipped to its fabric, anglers carry a large number of tools, accessories, and gadgets which, while perhaps not absolutely essential, definitely make for more enjoyable angling. There are hundreds of items to choose from, but certainly no fly fisherman should be without: a $\frac{1}{8}$ normal size matchbook to place next to fish prior to taking a picture; a pocket blowtorch or one of those little battery powered chain saws for cutting through tough tangles; a set of false-nose-and-eyebrow glasses for a quick disguise during embarrassing mishaps on one's home grounds; a pocket dictionary of epithets, either the classic *Blue Streak Handbook* or *Corwin's 1,001 Streamside Imprecations*; a couple of brush grenades to get your line loose from undergrowth on the opposite bank; a floating, glow-in-the-dark martini shaker; a box of irresistible, but highly laxative Trout Whammies or Salmon Blasters to drop in the water by the handful to punish uncooperative fish; a tube of fast-acting but easily removable Bailiff Baffler wicker glue to cement shut an incriminating creel; and one of the patented "just one more hour" stopwatches that sounds a soothing chime after 21 minutes.

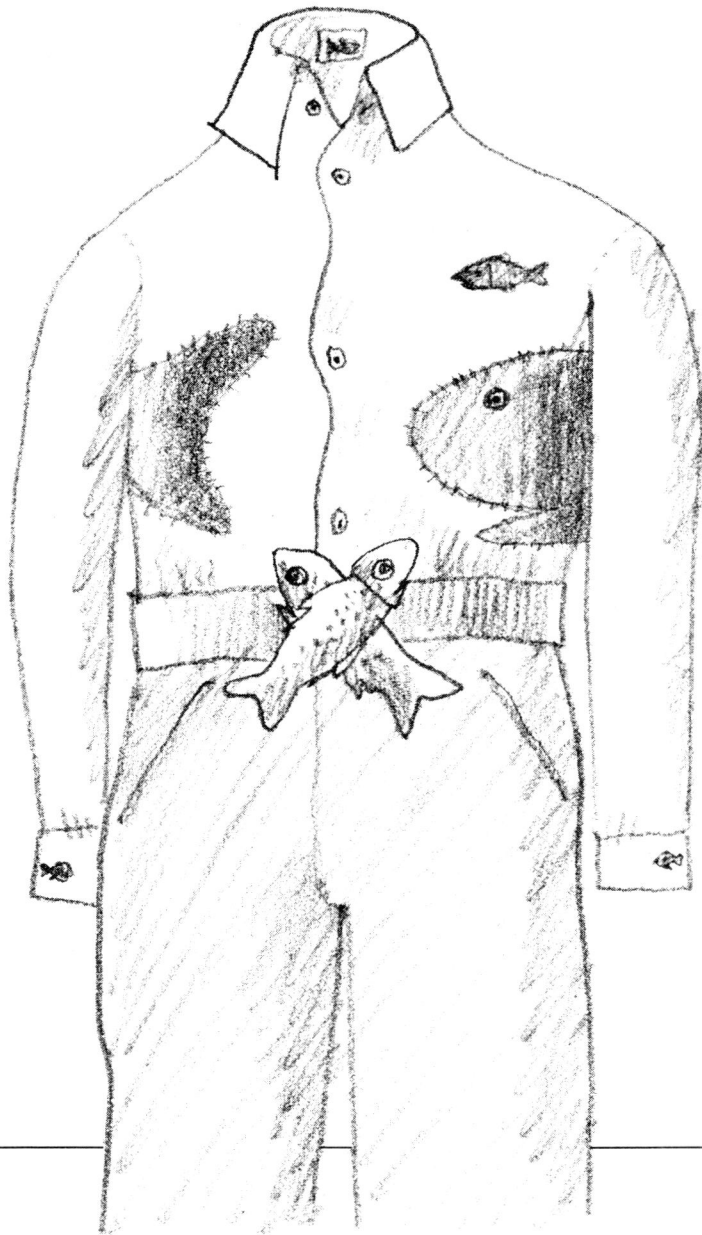

Waistcoat (Matching Accessories)

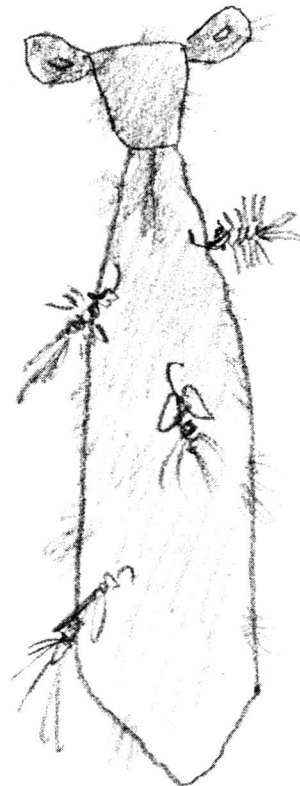

Walton (Carrying on the Great Tradition)

Walton, Isaak

Although it was really his younger associate, Charles Cotton, who provided the most enduring practical fishing advice, Walton has had by far the more lasting influence on the art of angling because of the lyrical quality of the prose he used to communicate his passion for fishing. One short example of his poetic discourse will suffice to illustrate the charming style that has earned for *The Compleat Angler* so reliable an audience from generation to generation:

And when you prepare to spin out a tale, see that your hands do not tremble, nor your eyes dart to and fro, and do not permit your hands to wander hither and thither, but hold the one carelessly over your heart, as if proclaiming an oath, and the other open in front of you, as if to say, 'See, I conceal nothing.' And when you commence to speak, take a great care to do so in a voice neither excessively loud, nor over-much meek, for just as you would not choose to drive a small nail with a sledge, or a bolt with a muffin, so too must you suit the tone to the purpose. And as to the contents of your little story, be guided thus: expand, but do not entirely invent. It is blasphemy and pure folly to usurp the role of the Creator and cause to appear upon the waters some imaginary monster which, perchance, snatched away your pole, made mincemeat of your leggings, mouthed a pony, and bore away your luggage on its back. But if you gently take one of His trout, and in a spirit of generous indulgence cause it to gain a foot or two of extra measure in the course of the telling, you will have the favour of your listeners, for truly the most mammoth specimen of a fish with which men are acquainted is far easier to swallow, as it were, than the tiniest exemplar of one yet unseen.

Water Release

The periodic release of impounded water into downstream areas by the managers of irrigation dams is announced by a series of siren signals. Anglers should be alert for these warnings and leave the stream immediately on hearing

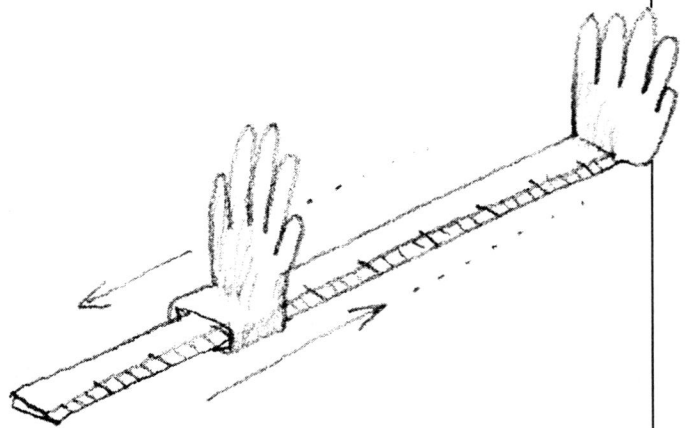

Yard

them. Incidentally, devices which mimic the sounds of these sirens are available "under the counter" at tackle shops. Ask for a Hoot 'n' Scoot or a De-Krowder.

Wrist — In an angler, the ache that connects the cuts and sores to the pulls and strains.

X

X. — Symbol for hybrid. A great deal of work has been done crossbreeding fish, notably trout, salmon, and char, to produce new strains and improved fishing. There have been a few successes, like the splake and the tiger trout, but most of the hybrids are short-lived, infertile, or genetically unstable. Somewhat more promising have been the occasional dramatic improvements in fishermen that have appeared due to accidental crosses. In England, for example, the common incidence of intermarriage between Episcopal bishops and female anglers has produced a number of good-natured and totally honest Bishermen. In Florida, there have been reports of a few Comp Trollers, the patient, meticulous, and rather dull result of a match between a deep sea fishing enthusiast and a certified public accountant. And in Massachusetts, trained observers have spotted the unmistakable progeny of unions between dedicated anglers and woman attorneys—the methodical, dextrous, and unbelievably devious Anglawyer.

Y

Yard — Unit of measurement. In angling, 17 inches.

Z

Zen Angling   It should come as no surprise that Zen, the noted Japanese Buddhist sect devoted to patient meditation and total concentration, produced not only students devoted to the practice of archery, but also adherents of the equally demanding art of angling. The father of Zen fishing was the monk Takesushi (1514?-1588?), who perfected the use of the bunku, a fishing apparatus of such subtlety that it would put even the great contemporary purist to shame. It consisted solely of a rare variety of silkworm specially bred to eat bamboo leaves. In his greatest catch, Takesushi reported having set one of his prize specimens loose on a likely looking bamboo plant along a trout stream outside Kyoto in the spring of 1555. The voracious worm stripped the sapling bare, ending at its top, where in early fall it began to form a cocoon for the winter. The October wind blew the now dead bamboo stalk forward and wedged it in a picturesque rock whose aesthetic qualities and fortuitous position the sharp-eyed sage had spotted months earlier. The wind also knocked the silkworm loose and left it dangling over a quiet pool. Trying to spin its way to freedom, it lengthened the delicate silk filament on which it hung until it came to the surface of the water, whereupon it was seized by a 92-dyami (44-pound) trout, which Takesushi, who had timed his arrival to the minute, pulled from the stream with a delicate motion of the long bamboo pole.

Zen Lying   Spiritual discipline founded by the Zen monk Takesushi.

Zzzzzzz   *1.* Sound made by patient angler waiting for a bite. *2.* Sound made by insect about to deliver one.

Zzzzzzzzz

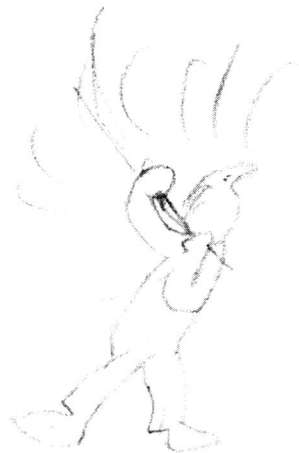
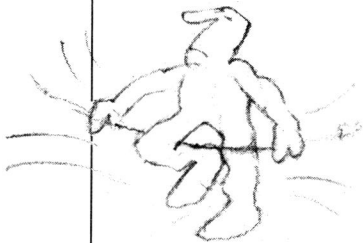